AF260754

Fun Fan Facts:
The Unofficial NBA Edition

Brooklyn Nets

Everything Young Nets
Fans Should Know

By: Jake Liam

Copyright © 2026 F3 Sports™ All rights reserved. ISBN: 978-1-972300-02-2

All characters, illustrations, and creative elements appearing in this work are original works developed under the creative direction of F3 Sports and are owned exclusively by F3 Sports.

This book is an unofficial guide and is not endorsed by, affiliated with, or sponsored by any official sports organization, league, or team. All trademarks and logos mentioned are the property of their respective owners. The artwork and illustrations contained in this book were created or adapted specifically for this publication and are intended to represent a parody or fictionalized version. They are not official team logos or affiliated imagery.

No part of this publication may be reproduced, distributed, or transmitted in any form or by any means, including photocopying, recording, or other electronic or mechanical methods, without the prior written permission of the publisher, except in the case of brief quotations embodied in critical reviews and certain other noncommercial uses permitted by copyright law.

Portions of the content and artwork in this book were generated with the assistance of artificial intelligence (AI) tools. All materials have been reviewed, edited, and curated by the author to ensure accuracy, originality, and alignment with the purpose of this publication.

Dedication

To every Nets fan who has stuck around through the name changes, the arena moves, the wild trades, and the "wait, we traded ALL our picks?" moments. Your loyalty is honestly kind of heroic.

And to Brooklyn. Because Brooklyn is not just a borough. It is an attitude.

THE NBA
BY THE NUMBERS

MOST NBA CHAMPIONSHIPS*

- CELTICS (18)
- LAKERS (17)
- WARRIORS (7)
- BULLS (6)
- SPURS (5)

As of the 2024-25 Season. † One Trophy = 4 Championships.

NBA HISTORY SNAPSHOT

1946	1954	1979	2023
NBA Founded	Shot Clock Introduced	3-Point Line Added	NBA Cup Introduced

BIG NUMBERS

$156 million
Stephen Curry's est. earnings in the 24-25 season

7'7"
Tallest player in NBA history (Gheorghe Mureșan & Manute Bol)

30 | 4 | 82

- **30** Teams Competing in the NBA
- **4** Playoff Rounds
- **82** Games Per Season

BROOKLYN NETS
IN THE NBA

- FOUNDED: 1976 †
- NBA TITLES: 0
- CONFERENCE TITLES: 2*

30 Playoff Appearances

*† Founding dates are complicated & may cause arguments at Thanksgiving. Ask someone born before color TV. All Titles reflect pre-relocation franchise history. * As of 2024-25 Season.*

NBA ALL-TIME MVP LEADERS

KAREEM ABDUL-JABBAR (6) ★ MICHAEL JORDAN (5) ★ BILL RUSSELL (5)

EASTERN CONFERENCE

- Atlantic – **Celtics**
- Atlantic – **Nets**
- Atlantic – **Knicks**
- Atlantic – **76ers**
- Atlantic – **Raptors**
- Central – **Bulls**
- Central – **Cavaliers**
- Central – **Pistons**
- Central – **Pacers**
- Central – **Bucks**
- Southeast – **Hawks**
- Southeast – **Hornets**
- Southeast – **Heat**
- Southeast – **Magic**
- Southeast – **Wizards**

WESTERN CONFERENCE

- Pacific – **Lakers**
- Pacific – **Clippers**
- Pacific – **Warriors**
- Pacific – **Suns**
- Pacific – **Kings**
- Northwest – **Nuggets**
- Northwest – **Timberwolves**
- Northwest – **Thunder**
- Northwest – **Trail Blazers**
- Northwest – **Jazz**
- Southwest – **Mavericks**
- Southwest – **Rockets**
- Southwest – **Spurs**
- Southwest – **Pelicans**
- Southwest – **Grizzlies**

Introduction

Welcome, fans! Whether you're new to cheering for the Brooklyn Nets or you've been bleeding the team colors your whole life, this book is packed with fun, exciting facts about your favorite team. Get ready to impress your friends and family with everything you know about the Nets.

Quick Time Out

This book is packed with stats. Like, A LOT of stats. Every fact was checked, double-checked, and triple-checked. But here's the thing about basketball history: not everyone agrees on everything. Ask someone who watched games before color TV and someone who grew up with instant replay and you'll get two completely different answers. My dad, stepdad, uncle, and grandpa all argued about the same fact. Four people. Four answers. All of them think they're right. So if you spot something that doesn't match what you've heard, congratulations. You might be a bigger fan than the people who helped make this book. And honestly? That's pretty cool.

HOW IT WORKS

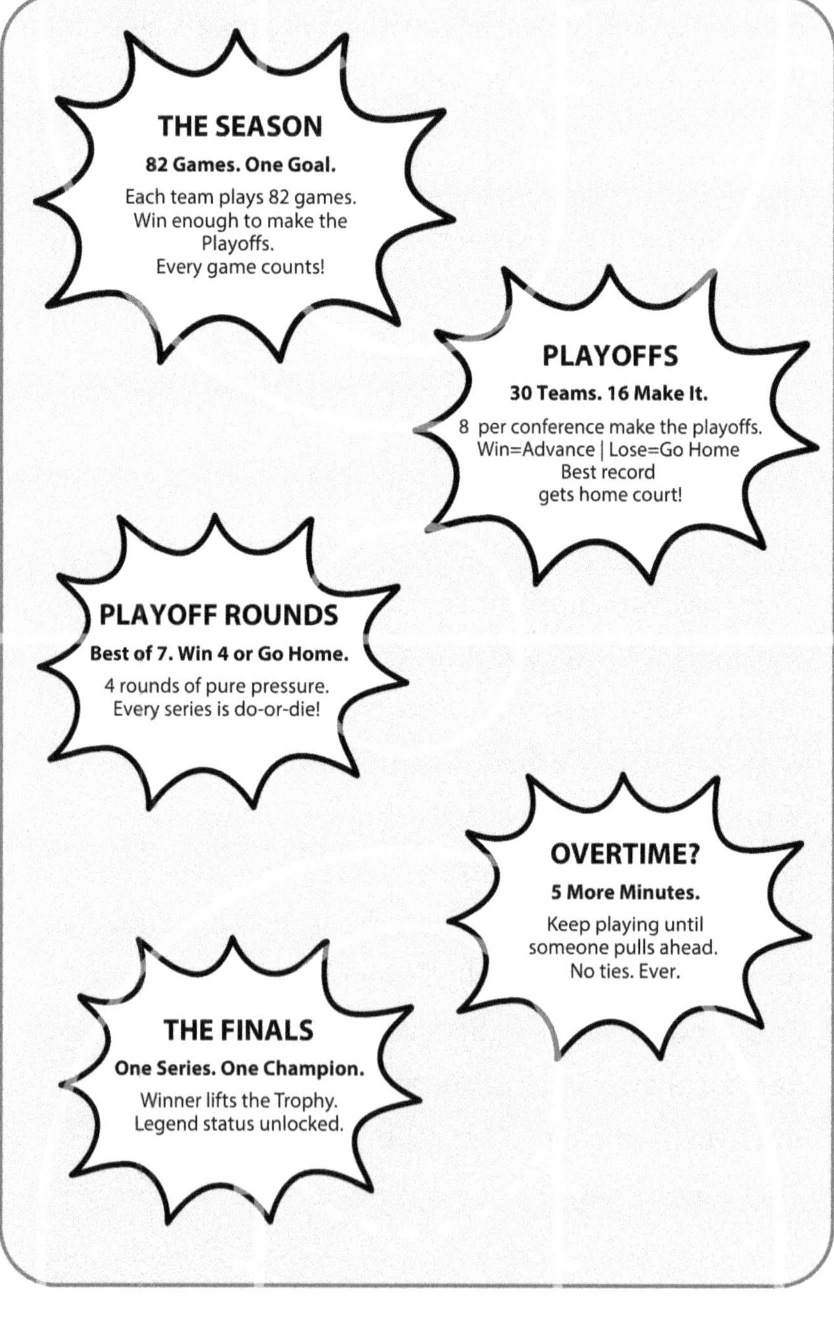
THE SEASON
82 Games. One Goal.
Each team plays 82 games.
Win enough to make the
Playoffs.
Every game counts!
PLAYOFFS
30 Teams. 16 Make It.
8 per conference make the playoffs.
Win=Advance | Lose=Go Home
Best record
gets home court!
PLAYOFF ROUNDS
Best of 7. Win 4 or Go Home.
4 rounds of pure pressure.
Every series is do-or-die!
OVERTIME?
5 More Minutes.
Keep playing until
someone pulls ahead.
No ties. Ever.
THE FINALS
One Series. One Champion.
Winner lifts the Trophy.
Legend status unlocked.

How the NBA Works

At first glance, basketball feels simple. Ten players. One ball. Two hoops. Go.

Then the NBA adds the layers.

An 82-game regular season. A draft where bad teams pick first. Playoffs that last two full months. Superstars who can change everything with one trade. Dynasties that rise, fall, and rise again.

And somehow, it all works.

The NBA is built on one big idea: every team gets a chance to reset, reload, and rise again. No relegation. No dropping down to a lower league. Just basketball, every night, from October through June.

It is a league designed for drama, stars, and comebacks. And once you understand the flow, it is impossible to stop watching.

The League Setup

The NBA has 30 teams, spread across the United States and Canada. Those teams are split into two conferences:

- Eastern Conference
- Western Conference

Each conference has three divisions, mostly based on geography. Divisions matter for scheduling, but not as much as they used to.

Every team plays 82 regular season games, usually from October through April. Home games. Road games. Back-to-back nights. Long road trips. The season is a marathon before the sprint even starts.

Win games, and you climb the standings. Lose too many, and the pressure builds fast.

How Games Are Played

An NBA game has four quarters, each lasting 12 minutes. That means 48 minutes of game time, plus timeouts, free throws, and the occasional coach argument that adds another 20 minutes nobody planned for.

Scoring is simple:

- A shot inside the three-point line is worth 2 points
- A shot beyond the arc is worth 3 points
- Free throws are worth 1 point

If the score is tied at the end of regulation, the game goes to overtime, which lasts 5 minutes. Still tied? Another overtime. Keep going until someone wins.

There is a shot clock too. Teams have 24 seconds to take a shot. No standing around. No holding the ball forever. Keep it moving.

The Regular Season Race

The regular season is long for a reason. It tests everything.

Depth. Health. Focus. Patience.

Teams play opponents from both conferences, but they face conference rivals more often. By the end of the season, each conference's top teams have earned their playoff spots the hard way.

The goal is simple: make the playoffs. But there is a twist.

The NBA Cup

In 2023, the NBA added something new to the middle of the season. Something with actual stakes. They called it the In-Season Tournament, now known as the NBA Cup.

It works like this: Every team plays a small group stage during November and December, with special court designs that look like nothing else in basketball. The best teams advance to a knockout round held in Las Vegas.

The winners split a prize pool. Players earn bonus money. And for the first time, a team could lift a trophy before the playoffs even started.

Some fans are still warming up to it. Some players love it. But the moment a team starts treating it seriously and a crowd shows up buzzing in December, it feels like something.

Which, honestly, sounds about right.

The Play-In Tournament

Instead of sending the top eight teams from each conference straight to the playoffs, the NBA added something new. The Play-In Tournament.

Here is how it works:

- Teams ranked 1 through 6 in each conference are safe
- Teams ranked 7 through 10 fight for the final two playoff spots

The 7 and 8 seeds have an advantage. Win once and you are in. Lose and you still get one more shot. The 9 and 10 seeds have to win twice in a row just to earn a first-round matchup.

It turns the end of the season into a sprint. Every game suddenly matters more. Fans love it. Coaches age rapidly.

The NBA Playoffs

Once the playoffs begin, everything tightens.

Sixteen teams enter. Eight from each conference. Every round is a best-of-seven games series. That means the first team to win four games moves on:

- First Round
- Conference Semifinals
- Conference Finals
- NBA Finals

Home-court advantage matters. Crowds get louder. Rotations get shorter. Superstars play heavier minutes. One bad quarter can flip a series. One great performance can define a career.

By the time the NBA Finals arrive in June, only two teams are left. One from the East. One from the West. Four wins away from a championship. Four wins away from history.

The NBA Draft: Hope Begins Here

Here is where the NBA gets clever. Every summer, new players enter the league through the NBA Draft. Teams take turns selecting college players, international stars, and teenagers straight out of high school.

The teams that finished with the worst records get the best odds to pick early through the Draft Lottery. It is not guaranteed, but it gives struggling franchises a real shot at changing their future with one pick.

That means one bad season does not doom you forever. It might actually change everything. Some franchises are rebuilt by a single draft night moment.

Hope shows up wearing a new jersey.

No Relegation. All Pressure.

Unlike many global sports leagues, NBA teams never drop down to a lower league. They always stay in the NBA.

That does not mean there is no pressure.

Fans remember losing seasons. Owners make changes. Coaches get replaced. Players get traded. Every year is a test of direction, patience, and belief.

Stars, Systems, and Showtime

The NBA is famous for its stars. But stars do not win alone.

Teams need chemistry. Coaches need systems. Role players need to deliver on the biggest stages. One injury. One hot streak. One trade deadline deal. Any of it can flip a season.

That balance between individual brilliance and team basketball is what makes the league special.

Fast breaks. Buzzer-beaters. Game 7s. And moments that get replayed forever. That is the NBA.

Once you get the flow, it is pure electricity.

Brooklyn Nets Facts

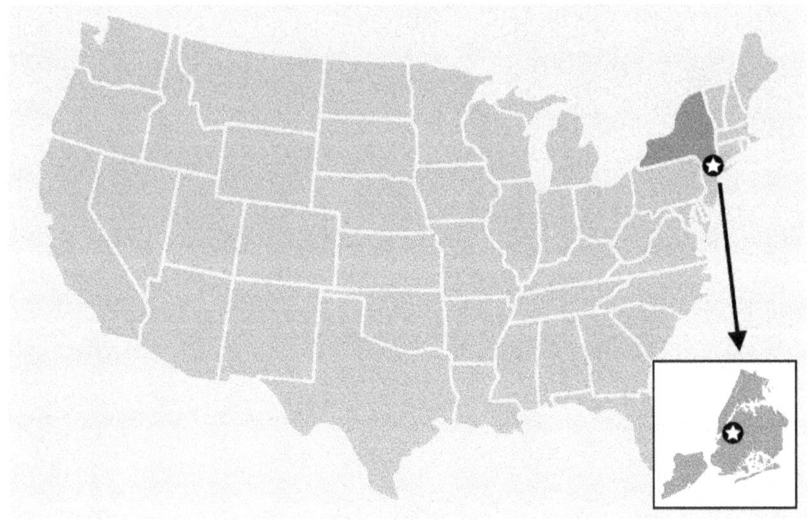

Home City

Brooklyn, New York

Metro Area Population

About 20 Million

Home Arena

Barclays Center

Arena Capacity

17,732

Conference / Division

Eastern Conference / Atlantic Division

Famous Local Food

NY-Style Pizza, Bagels, Cheesecake, Street Cart Hot Dogs

1. Born in the ABA: The Wildest League You Have Never Heard Of (1967)

The Brooklyn Nets were not always the Brooklyn Nets. They were not always in Brooklyn. They were not even always in the NBA. The franchise started in 1967 as the New Jersey Americans, playing in the American Basketball Association, a rival league of the NBA in the 1960s and 70s. It was basically the NBA's wild younger sibling who showed up to the party wearing a red, white, and blue basketball and refused to follow anyone's rules.

The ABA was chaos in the best way possible. Three-point lines before the NBA had them. Slam dunk contests. A multi-coloured basketball that looked like it belonged at a Fourth of July barbecue. The league was flashy, fun, and a little bit nuts. And right in the middle of it were the Americans, trying to figure out who they were and where they belonged.

That first season was rough. The team played in Teaneck, New Jersey, at an armory that was about as glamorous as it sounds. Attendance was low. Wins were rare. But the franchise survived, which is honestly the most important part of the early Nets story. They did not have championships or superstars yet. They just had stubbornness. And sometimes that is enough to keep the lights on until the good stuff arrives.

2. From Americans to Nets: Decades in the Garden State

The franchise changed its name more times in its first few years than most teams change their jerseys. They started as the New Jersey Americans in 1967. One year later, they became the New York Nets. Then after the ABA-NBA merger in 1976, the team settled into New Jersey and became the New Jersey Nets. And that is where they stayed. For a long time.

From 1977 to 2012, the Nets were a New Jersey team. Thirty-five years. That is not a pit stop. That is a home. They played at the Brendan Byrne Arena in East Rutherford for most of that stretch. Generations of fans grew up driving to the Meadowlands on game nights, sitting in those seats, and calling this their team. The Nets were not some temporary tenant in Jersey. They were part of the fabric.

So why "Nets" in the first place? The story goes that ownership wanted a name that rhymed with the other big New York-area sports teams: the Mets (baseball) and the Jets (football). Mets, Jets, Nets. Catchy, easy to remember, and it has absolutely nothing to do with actual basketball nets, even though that worked out as a happy coincidence. The name survived every era, every arena, and every identity crisis the franchise went through. In a history full of change, "Nets" was the one thing that never left.

3. Julius Erving and the ABA Glory Days (1973-1976)

Before the Nets had any NBA history, they had Julius Erving. And honestly? That was more than enough. Dr. J, as everyone called him, was the most electrifying basketball player alive. He could fly. He could dunk from places that did not seem physically possible. He played above the rim in an era when most players were still figuring out what the rim was for.

Erving joined the Nets in 1973, and the effect was immediate. He was like a superhero who decided to suit up for your local team. The Nets went from struggling to survive to winning ABA championships in 1974 and 1976. Dr. J won three MVP awards in his time with the

Nets and put on a show every single night that made fans forget they were watching a league most people had never heard of.

The ABA was the perfect stage for Erving. The league celebrated style, creativity, and showmanship, and Dr. J had all three cranked up to eleven. His dunks were not just athletic. They were artistic. He would take off from the free throw line, hang in the air for what felt like three full seconds, and finish with a slam that shook the backboard. In an era before social media, before YouTube, before highlight reels on your phone, people still knew about Dr. J. He was that good. And for a few magical years, he belonged to the Nets.

Dr. J, Air Traffic Warning. Julius Erving flew to the basket long before today's high-flying stars. With the New York Nets, Dr. J turned fast breaks into takeoff runs and the rim into a landing pad. Defenders could only watch and hope he missed. *Photo: Julius Erving with the New York Nets. Source: Wikimedia Commons.*

4. The Painful NBA Merger: Selling Dr. J Just to Survive (1976)

In 1976, the ABA and the NBA finally merged. Four ABA teams were absorbed into the NBA: the Nets, the Denver Nuggets, the Indiana Pacers, and the San Antonio Spurs. Sounds great, right? Bigger stage. More money. More exposure. There was just one gigantic, heartbreaking problem.

The NBA charged each ABA team a merger fee to join the league. For the Nets, that fee was $3.2 million. On top of that, they had to pay an additional $4.8 million to the New York Knicks for "territorial rights," basically a fee for existing in the same market. The Nets' owner did not have that kind of cash. So he did the unthinkable. He sold Julius Erving to the Philadelphia 76ers.

Let that sink in. The Nets had to sell the best player in basketball just to afford the entry fee. It would be like winning the lottery and then having to give the ticket away to pay for the gas to drive to the lottery office. Nets fans were devastated. Dr. J went on to become an NBA legend in Philly while the Nets started their NBA life in New Jersey with an empty roster and an empty wallet. It was the worst trade in franchise history at the time. Spoiler alert: it would not be the last time the Nets made a deal that haunted them.

5. From Jersey to Brooklyn: The Move That Split the Fan Base (2012)

For thirty-five years, the Nets were New Jersey's team. Not New York's. Not Brooklyn's. Jersey's. Fans drove to the Meadowlands. They wore New Jersey across their chests. They sat through losing seasons, celebrated the Jason Kidd Finals runs, and stuck with the team when nobody else in the country was paying attention. That loyalty was real, and it ran deep.

Then in 2012, the franchise packed up and moved to the Barclays Center in Brooklyn. New arena. New borough. New colors. New everything. For the ownership group and the national media, it was exciting. A fresh start in the biggest city on Earth. For New Jersey fans who had been riding with this team for decades? It felt like getting dumped. Some fans made the trip across the river and kept cheering. Others could not stomach rooting for a Brooklyn team after years of repping Jersey. The split was real, and it was painful.

Here is the thing that makes it complicated. The move gave the Nets something they never truly had: a permanent identity. In New Jersey, the team always felt overshadowed, stuck in the shadow of the Knicks and fighting for attention in a market that treated them like an afterthought. In Brooklyn, they became the borough's team almost overnight. Jay-Z. The Biggie connection. The black-and-white rebrand. Suddenly the Nets were cool in a way they had never been before. But "cool" does not erase thirty-five years of history, and there are still fans in New Jersey who remember exactly what it felt like when their team left. Every franchise move has two sides. The side that gains a team, and the side that loses one. Both matter.

6. Julius Erving (1973-1976): The Player Who Changed How Basketball Looks

We already talked about what Dr. J did for the Nets in Chapter 1. Now let us talk about what he did for basketball itself. Because Julius Erving did not just play the game. He reinvented it. Before Dr. J, basketball was mostly played below the rim. Guys dribbled, passed, shot jumpers, and occasionally dunked. Erving turned the area above the rim into his personal office.

His dunks were not normal. He would take off from impossible distances, twist his body in midair, and finish with slams that made people in the stands literally stand up and scream. His most famous move, the baseline reverse layup where he went under the backboard and somehow put the ball in from the other side, is still considered one of the greatest plays in basketball history. He did not learn that from a coaching manual. He invented it in real time.

What makes Erving's Nets years so special is that he did all of this in the ABA, a league that most casual fans have forgotten. He was a superstar performing on a small stage. When he finally got to the NBA with the Sixers, the whole world saw what Nets fans already knew. Dr. J was not just ahead of his time. He was the blueprint for every high-flying player who came after him. Michael Jordan, Vince Carter, LeBron James. They all owe a little something to the guy who did it first in a Nets jersey.

7. Jason Kidd (2001-2008): The Floor General Who Changed Everything

Jason Kidd arrived in New Jersey in 2001 via trade from the Phoenix Suns, and the transformation was immediate. The Nets went from a team nobody talked about to a team nobody could ignore. Kidd did not do it by scoring 30 points a night. He did it by making every single person around him better.

Kidd was a point guard who saw the game three passes ahead of everyone else. He would grab a rebound, push the ball up the court at full speed, and deliver a pass so perfect that his teammates barely had to move their hands to catch it. He led the league in assists multiple times, racked up triple-doubles like they were participation trophies, and played defense with a nastiness that most point guards did not bother with.

In his first season with the Nets, Kidd led the team to the NBA Finals. His second season? Back to the Finals again. Back-to-back Eastern Conference championships for a franchise that had been irrelevant for years. The Nets lost both Finals series, but Kidd had single-handedly turned the franchise into a contender and gave New Jersey fans something they had not felt in a long time: pride. He proved that one player, if he is smart enough and tough enough, can change the entire direction of a franchise overnight.

8. Brook Lopez (2008-2017): Mr. Brooklyn (and Mr. New Jersey Before That)

Brook Lopez might not be the most famous name on this list, but to Nets fans, he is one of the most beloved. Lopez was drafted 10th overall in 2008 and spent nine seasons with the franchise, playing through some of the toughest years in team history. He was there for the final New Jersey seasons. He was there for the move to Brooklyn. He was there when the arena was shiny and new. He was there when the roster around him was not great.

Lopez was a skilled seven-footer with a soft touch around the basket and a personality that made him impossible not to like. He loved comic books, had a thing for visiting Disneyland, and once got into a public debate with his twin brother Robin about which Disney park was better. He was the kind of player who kept showing up, kept putting up numbers, and kept the fan base entertained even when the wins were hard to find.

What makes Lopez special is loyalty. He could have complained about losing. He could have forced a trade. Instead, he represented the Nets with class and consistency for nearly a decade. For fans who lived through the rough years, Brook Lopez was the Nets. He might not have a championship ring from Brooklyn, but he has something just as rare in professional sports: genuine love from a fan base that will never forget him.

9. Vince Carter (2004-2009): Half-Man, Half-Amazing Lands in New Jersey

When Vince Carter arrived in New Jersey via trade from the Toronto Raptors in 2004, the Nets suddenly had something they had not had since Dr. J: a player who could make your jaw literally drop. Carter was one of the most spectacular dunkers in NBA history. His nickname was "Half-Man, Half-Amazing" and honestly, that might have been underselling it.

Carter had already cemented his legend by winning the 2000 NBA Slam Dunk Contest with a performance that is still considered the greatest dunk contest of all time. He famously dunked over a 7-foot-2 defender during the 2000 Olympics. Over him. Like the guy was not even there. When he got to New Jersey, he brought that same electricity to a fan base that desperately needed some excitement.

With the Nets, Carter became the go-to scorer and the reason people actually tuned into games. He could shoot threes, drive to the basket, and of course, throw down dunks that made the highlight reels every single night. The Nets made the playoffs multiple times during Carter's tenure. They never won a championship, but Carter gave the franchise credibility and gave fans a reason to buy tickets. In a stretch where the Nets were fighting for attention in a market dominated by the Knicks, having Vince Carter was like having a neon sign that said, "Hey, we are over here, and we are exciting."

10. Buck Williams (1981-1989): The Workhorse Who Never Quit

Buck Williams was drafted 3rd overall by the Nets in 1981, and what he walked into was not pretty. The Nets were one of the worst teams in the NBA. The roster was thin. The arena was half-empty most nights. The future looked about as bright as a broken flashlight. A lot of young players would have mentally checked out. Buck Williams did the exact opposite.

Williams was named Rookie of the Year in his first season, which is impressive for anyone but especially impressive when your team is losing almost every night. He was a power forward who did all the dirty work: rebounding, defending, setting screens, diving for loose balls. He was not flashy. He did not make highlight reels. He just showed up every single game and outworked whoever was standing across from him.

For eight seasons, Williams was the one constant on a Nets roster that kept changing around him. He made All-Star teams. He grabbed rebounds by the truckload. He gave the franchise credibility during years when credibility was hard to come by. Williams eventually left for the Portland Trail Blazers, where he continued his career at a high level. But Nets fans from that era remember him as the guy who kept the faith when there was not much to be faithful about. Every franchise needs a Buck Williams at some point. Someone who does not care about the circumstances and just plays.

11. Dr. J's ABA Championships: When the Nets Ruled Their World (1974, 1976)

Before the Nets ever played a single NBA game, they were champions. Twice. In the ABA, the Nets won titles in 1974 and 1976, and both times, Julius Erving was the reason the trophy came home.

The 1974 championship was the franchise's first taste of glory. Dr. J was a scoring machine, flying through the air and dunking on anyone brave enough to stand in his way. The Nets beat the Utah Stars in five games, and Erving was named playoff MVP. The celebration was real, even if most of America was not paying attention. The ABA was still the "other league." But for Nets fans? It did not matter. A championship is a championship, and this one was theirs.

The 1976 title was even sweeter. The Nets swept the Denver Nuggets in four games, with Erving putting on an absolute masterclass. He averaged over 34 points per game in the series. Thirty-four. In a sweep. That is not just winning. That is embarrassing the other team while looking cool doing it. The 1976 championship turned out to be the last great moment of the ABA, because the league merged with the NBA later that year. The Nets went out as champions. Not a bad way to close a chapter.

12. Jason Kidd Takes the Nets to the NBA Finals: Nobody Saw This Coming (2002)

Let us set the scene. The year is 2002. The New Jersey Nets have been a punchline for most of their NBA existence. They have not won a playoff series in years. The arena is half-empty. National media pretends they do not exist. Then Jason Kidd shows up and says, "Nah. We are doing this."

Kidd had arrived via trade from Phoenix the previous summer, and the results were instant. The Nets went from 26 wins the year before to 52 wins. Kidd was dishing assists like he had GPS tracking on every teammate. He pushed the pace, created fast breaks out of thin air, and turned role players into confident scorers. The Nets ripped through the Eastern Conference playoffs and suddenly found themselves in the NBA Finals against the Los Angeles Lakers.

They lost to the Lakers in four games. Shaq and Kobe were a problem nobody could solve that year. But the loss did not erase what the Nets had accomplished. This franchise, this forgotten, arena-hopping, punchline franchise, was playing for a championship. Kidd had taken a team from the basement to the Finals in one season. The Nets went back to the Finals in 2003 too, losing to the San Antonio Spurs. Two straight Finals trips. For the New Jersey Nets. If you had bet on that happening, you would have been a very rich person, because nobody else on Earth saw it coming.

13. Drazen Petrovic: The Shooting Star Gone Too Soon (1991-1993)

Some Nets stories are about championships. Some are about wild trades. This one is about a player who burned so bright that his legacy lasted forever, even though his time was painfully short.

Drazen Petrovic came to the Nets from the Portland Trail Blazers in 1991. He was born in Sibenik, Croatia, and had already become a legend in European basketball before coming to the NBA. When he arrived in New Jersey, he had something to prove. European players were not taken seriously in the NBA back then. Coaches doubted them. Fans dismissed them. Petrovic did not care about any of that. He just started scoring.

Petrovic had one of the purest shooting strokes anyone had ever seen. He averaged over 22 points per game in his final full season, hitting jumpers from everywhere on the court with a confidence that made defenders look helpless. He was fierce, competitive, and played with a fire that Nets fans had not seen in years. Then on June 7, 1993, Drazen Petrovic was killed in a car accident in Germany. He was 28 years old. The basketball world was stunned. The Nets retired his number 3 jersey, and his legacy paved the way for every European player who came to the NBA after him. Guys like Dirk Nowitzki, Tony Parker, and Luka Doncic all walked through a door that Drazen Petrovic helped open. He did not get enough time. But the time he had mattered more than most careers that last twenty years.

14. Kevin Durant and Kyrie Irving Arrive: The Hype Was Unreal (2019)

In the summer of 2019, the Brooklyn Nets pulled off something that seemed impossible. Kevin Durant, one of the greatest scorers in NBA history, and Kyrie Irving, one of the most talented point guards alive, both signed with the Nets as free agents. Two superstars. One team. Brooklyn. The basketball world collectively gasped.

The hype was through the roof. Durant was coming off winning two championships with the Golden State Warriors. Kyrie had hit one of the biggest shots in NBA history to win the 2016 title with Cleveland. Together, on paper, they were supposed to turn Brooklyn into an instant championship contender. Add James Harden later via trade, and the Nets had three former MVPs on the same roster. Three. People were already penciling them in for the Finals.

And then it got complicated. Durant missed his entire first season recovering from an Achilles injury. When the Big Three finally played together, injuries and chemistry issues kept pulling them apart. Kyrie missed significant time. Harden wanted out and was traded to Philadelphia. The drama was louder than the wins. The

Nets made the playoffs but never reached the Finals. By 2023, Durant was traded to Phoenix and Kyrie went to Dallas. The Brooklyn superteam era ended not with a bang but with a very loud, very dramatic whimper. It was proof that talent alone does not win championships. You need chemistry. You need health. And you need everyone pulling in the same direction.

15. The Infamous Boston Trade: The Deal That Haunts the Nets (2013)

Okay. Deep breath. This one hurts.

In the summer of 2013, the Brooklyn Nets traded a massive package of future draft picks to the Boston Celtics in exchange for veteran stars Paul Pierce and Kevin Garnett. The idea was simple: Pierce and Garnett were proven champions. Pair them with the Nets' existing roster, and Brooklyn would compete for a title immediately. Win now. Worry about the future later.

The problem? "Later" showed up fast. Pierce and Garnett were both on the wrong side of 30. They were still good players, but they were not the same guys who won the championship in 2008. The Nets lost in the second round of the 2014 playoffs. That was the high point. After that, Pierce left. Garnett was traded. And all those draft picks the Nets had sent to Boston? They turned into some very good players. One of those picks became Jayson Tatum. Another became Jaylen Brown. You know, the two guys who just won the 2024 championship for the Celtics. With the Nets' picks.

The trade is widely considered one of the worst in NBA history. The Nets spent years without their own first-round draft picks, unable to rebuild properly while the Celtics used Brooklyn's picks to build a champion. It was like paying for someone else's house and then watching them throw a party in it. Nets fans still wince when you bring it up. The lesson? "Win now" only works if you actually win.

16. The Jay-Z Connection and the Brooklyn Brand

The story of the Nets moving to Brooklyn cannot be told without talking about Jay-Z. Shawn Carter, better known as one of the greatest rappers alive, was born and raised in Brooklyn. When the idea of bringing an NBA team to the borough first came up, Jay-Z became a minority owner of the Nets and one of the loudest voices pushing the move forward.

Jay-Z did not just invest money. He invested credibility. When one of the most famous musicians on the planet says Brooklyn needs a basketball team, people listen. He helped shape the team's black-and-white color scheme, performed at the Barclays Center's opening, and turned the Nets into something they had never been before: cool. For the first time in franchise history, wearing a Nets hat was a fashion statement, not a conversation starter about why you were not wearing a Knicks hat instead.

Jay-Z eventually sold his ownership stake, but his fingerprints are still all over the franchise. The Brooklyn Nets' identity, the sleek design, the hip-hop connection, the borough pride, all traces back to the moment Jay-Z decided to make this happen. Not bad for a kid from the Marcy Projects.

17. Brooklyn vs. Manhattan: Why the Borough Matters

Here is something people who are not from New York might not understand: Brooklyn is not Manhattan. They are both part of New York City, but they are completely different worlds. Manhattan has the skyscrapers, Times Square, and Wall Street. Brooklyn has brownstones, street art, and an attitude that says, "We do things our own way over here."

Brooklyn is the most populated borough in New York City, with about 2.7 million people. If it were its own city, it would be the third-largest in the United States. It has its own culture, its own food scene, its own music history, and its own fierce sense of pride. When you tell someone from Brooklyn where you are from, you do not say "New York." You say "Brooklyn." That distinction matters.

For the Nets, being Brooklyn's team means being part of that identity. The Knicks are Manhattan's team. The bright lights. Madison Square Garden. Celebrity row.

The Nets are the borough's team. Grittier. Less flashy. But just as proud. It is a different kind of fan base, one that values authenticity over glamor and loyalty over hype. When you see someone wearing a Nets jersey in Brooklyn, they are not just supporting a basketball team. They are repping their neighborhood. And in Brooklyn, the neighborhood is everything.

18. The Coogi Sweater Jerseys and Nets Fashion Game

In 2019, the Brooklyn Nets released a City Edition jersey that instantly became one of the coolest in NBA history. The design was inspired by the colorful Coogi sweaters made famous by Brooklyn legend The Notorious B.I.G. (Biggie Smalls), who rapped about Coogi so often that the brand became synonymous with his name. The jersey featured the same bright, wavy patterns in a tribute that was equal parts fashion and hip-hop history.

The reaction was electric. Fans bought them out almost immediately. People who did not even watch basketball wanted one. The jersey captured something that the Nets had been building since moving to Brooklyn: a connection to the borough's culture that went deeper than just basketball. Biggie was Brooklyn royalty. The

Coogi sweater was his signature. Putting that on a basketball jersey was genius.

The Nets have continued to lean into fashion and culture with their jersey designs, releasing City Edition uniforms that reference Brooklyn's street art scene, graffiti culture, and neighborhood identity. In a league where jersey drops have become almost as big as game nights, the Nets have quietly become one of the best-dressed teams in the NBA. Who knew the team that used to play in the New Jersey Meadowlands would become a fashion icon?

19. Sharing New York with the Knicks: The Battle for the City

Let us be honest. Playing second fiddle to the New York Knicks for decades was not easy. The Knicks have Madison Square Garden. They have the history. They have Spike Lee in the front row. For most of the Nets' existence, being a Nets fan in New York meant constantly being asked, "Wait, why are you not a Knicks fan?"

The rivalry between the Nets and the Knicks is not like the Celtics-Lakers rivalry. It is not built on decades of Finals battles. It is more like a sibling rivalry where the older sibling gets all the attention and the younger one has to work twice as hard to be noticed. The Nets have spent years trying to carve out their own identity in a city where the Knicks owned the basketball conversation.

But here is the thing: the Nets have actually had more recent success than the Knicks in many stretches. Jason Kidd took the Nets to back-to-back Finals when the Knicks were struggling. The Brooklyn move created buzz the Knicks had not felt in years. The KD and Kyrie signings made the Nets the hottest team in the city for a while. The battle for New York is not over. It might never be. But the Nets have proven that this city is big enough for two basketball teams, and Brooklyn is not going to apologize for showing up.

20. Barclays Center: More Than Just Basketball

The Barclays Center is not just where the Nets play basketball. It is one of the busiest entertainment venues in the entire country. Since opening in 2012, the arena has hosted everything from major concerts to boxing matches to pro wrestling events to college basketball tournaments. On any given week, you might see a Nets game on Tuesday, a Beyonce concert on Thursday, and a championship boxing match on Saturday. The building never sleeps.

The arena holds about 17,732 fans for basketball, making it smaller than a lot of NBA arenas. But that tight capacity actually works in the Nets' favor. The seats are close to the court. The acoustics are solid. When the crowd is into it, the noise wraps around you in a way that bigger arenas cannot match. It is intimate without feeling small.

What really makes Barclays special is the location. Step outside after a game and you are immediately in one of the most vibrant neighbourhoods in Brooklyn. Restaurants, shops, street performers, and the general buzz of Atlantic Avenue at night. Going to a Nets game is not just about the game. It is about the whole Brooklyn experience. Grab a slice before tip-off. Walk through the neighbourhood after the final buzzer. It is the kind of game night that makes you understand why the move to Brooklyn was the best thing that ever happened to this franchise.

21. The Rebuild Gets Real (2023-present)

After the Kevin Durant and Kyrie Irving era ended with trades instead of trophies, the Nets found themselves right back where they had been before: rebuilding. Again. It is a familiar feeling for this franchise. The superstars left. The spotlight faded. And the Nets had to figure out what comes next.

But here is the thing about rebuilds: they are not always a bad thing. Sometimes tearing it down and starting fresh is exactly what a team needs. The Nets entered the 2025-26 season with one of the youngest rosters in the league, full of players hungry to prove themselves. No massive egos. No drama. Just a group of guys trying to earn minutes, earn wins, and earn the trust of a fan base that has been through a lot.

Rebuilds are not glamorous. The wins do not always come. The standings are not always pretty. But every great team in NBA history went through a stretch where they were building something. The Celtics did it. The Warriors did it. The Bucks did it. The Nets have the pieces to start stacking. It just takes time, patience, and the right picks. And for the first time in a long time, the Nets actually have those picks.

22. The Flatbush Five: Five First-Round Picks in One Night (2025 NBA Draft)

Remember all those draft picks the Nets collected from the Mikal Bridges trade and other deals? In the 2025 NBA Draft, the Nets cashed them in. All of them. Brooklyn made five first-round selections in a single draft, something no NBA team had ever done before. Egor Demin went 8th overall. Nolan Traore went 19th. Drake Powell went 22nd. Ben Saraf went 26th. Danny Wolf went 27th. Five rookies. One draft night. Nets fans did not know whether to celebrate or panic. Most did both.

The reaction around the league was wild. The Phoenix Suns actually made fun of it on social media. Critics said the Nets were hoarding players they could not develop all at once. But Brooklyn had a plan. Throw a bunch of talented young guys into the fire, see who thrives, and build from there. The group quickly earned a nickname: the Flatbush Five. Demin emerged as a sharpshooting guard who hit nearly 39 percent of his threes as a rookie, which is ridiculous for a 19-year-old. Traore, the

French point guard, started slow but exploded in the second half of the season, averaging nearly 16 points and 7 assists over his best stretch and looking like a future starting point guard.

Not every pick will become a star. That is the reality of any draft class. But the Flatbush Five gave Brooklyn something it had not had in years: hope that was homegrown, not purchased. These were not rentals or free agent splashes. These were the Nets' own guys, learning together, growing together, and building something from scratch. For a franchise that spent years trading away its future, drafting five first-rounders in one night felt like the universe finally giving Brooklyn a do-over.

23. Mikal Bridges... Wait, Where Did He Go? (Traded 2024)

This one stings. Mikal Bridges came to the Nets in the Kevin Durant trade and was supposed to be a cornerstone of the rebuild. He was a two-way wing who could guard the best player on the other team and knock down open threes on offense. He played all 82 games every season. He was durable, reliable, and exactly the kind of player you build around.

Then in the summer of 2024, the Nets traded Bridges to the New York Knicks. Of all teams. The Knicks. Brooklyn's crosstown rival. The team that Nets fans spend half their energy arguing with. Bridges went across the city and became part of the Knicks' Villanova reunion with Jalen Brunson, Josh Hart, and Donte DiVincenzo.

For Nets fans, losing Bridges was tough. Losing him to the Knicks was tougher. But the Nets got back a haul of draft picks and young players that directly fueled the Flatbush Five draft. That trade is the reason Brooklyn had five first-round picks in 2025. It does not feel great to watch your guy put on a rival's jersey. But ask the Celtics how the "trade for future picks" strategy worked out after the 2013 deal. Sometimes the team that collects the picks ends up winning the war. The Nets are betting everything that history is about to repeat, this time in their favor.

24. Cam Thomas: The One That Got Away (2021-2026)

For four and a half seasons, Cam Thomas was the Nets' most exciting young scorer. Drafted 27th overall in 2021, Thomas had one elite skill that nobody could deny: the basketball went in when he shot it. He averaged 24 points per game in the 2023-24 season and had nights where he looked like the best scorer in the entire league. When Thomas got hot, there was no stopping him.

But the relationship between Thomas and the Nets slowly fell apart. Brooklyn could not agree on a long-term contract with him during the 2024 offseason. Thomas accepted a one-year qualifying offer, which was basically a placeholder deal that satisfied nobody. The 2025-26 season started rough. Hamstring injuries limited him to 24 games. His minutes shrunk. His role changed. And then, right at the February trade deadline, the Nets waived him. Just like that. The guy who had been their leading scorer was gone.

Thomas signed with the Milwaukee Bucks. It was a messy ending to a relationship that once had so much promise. For Nets fans, losing Thomas stung because they watched him grow from a second-round pick into a legitimate scoring threat. But the franchise decided to bet on the Flatbush Five and the rebuild instead. Whether that was the right call is a question that will not be answered for a few years. That is the hardest part of rebuilding. You do not get to know if you were right until later.

25. What Is Next for Brooklyn?

The Brooklyn Nets have been a lot of things over the years. ABA champions. New Jersey lifers. NBA nomads. Punchline. Contender. Superteam. Rebuild project. The franchise has reinvented itself more times than most teams change their court design. And now, heading into the next chapter, the question is simple: what does this team want to become?

The 2025-26 season has not been about wins and losses. At 15-40 and change, nobody is pretending otherwise. This season has been about development. Egor Demin proving he can shoot at the NBA level. Nolan Traore proving he can run an offense. Michael Porter Jr. providing a veteran presence. Coach Jordi Fernandez giving his young guys real minutes and real responsibility, even when the scoreboard is not cooperating. The foundation is being poured. The building comes later.

The NBA is a league where things can change fast. One great draft pick. One unexpected leap from a young player. One smart trade. And suddenly the Nets are back in the conversation. It has happened before. Jason Kidd turned this franchise around in one summer. The move to Brooklyn changed everything overnight. The Nets' history proves that when the right moment comes, this franchise knows how to seize it. So what is next? Nobody knows for sure. But if you are a Brooklyn Nets fan, you have already survived the worst trades, the weirdest arena moves, and the most dramatic roster implosions in NBA history. Whatever comes next, you can handle it. And somewhere in the future, there is a banner waiting. Brooklyn just has to go get it.

Bonus Trivia Quiz!

You think you are a true Nets fan? Try this bonus quiz!

1. What league did the Nets originally play in before joining the NBA?

A) The World Basketball League

B) The American Basketball Association (ABA)

C) The European Basketball League

D) The Continental Basketball Association

2. Why was the team named the "Nets"?

A) Because basketball has nets on the hoops

B) To rhyme with the Mets and Jets

C) It was the owner's last name

D) It was chosen in a fan contest

3. How many ABA championships did the Nets win with Julius Erving?

A) One

B) Two

C) Three

D) Four

4. Why did the Nets have to sell Julius Erving when they joined the NBA in 1976?

A) He wanted to play for a bigger market team
B) He was too old to keep playing
C) They needed money to pay the NBA merger fee
D) He failed a physical exam

5. Which Nets player was nicknamed "Half-Man, Half-Amazing"?

A) Jason Kidd
B) Vince Carter
C) Julius Erving
D) Brook Lopez

6. How many consecutive NBA Finals did Jason Kidd lead the Nets to in the early 2000s?

A) One
B) Two
C) Three
D) Four

7. What famous rapper was a minority owner of the Nets and helped push the move to Brooklyn?

A) Drake

B) Kanye West

C) Jay-Z

D) Nas

8. What year did the Nets officially move to the Barclays Center in Brooklyn?

A) 2008

B) 2010

C) 2012

D) 2015

9. Which Brooklyn hip-hop legend inspired the Nets' famous Coogi sweater City Edition jerseys?

A) Jay-Z

B) The Notorious B.I.G.

C) Lil Kim

D) Busta Rhymes

10. In the infamous 2013 trade, the Nets sent future draft picks to which team in exchange for Paul Pierce and Kevin Garnett?

A) Los Angeles Lakers

B) Chicago Bulls

C) Boston Celtics

D) Miami Heat

11. Which two superstars signed with the Nets as free agents in 2019?

A) LeBron James and Anthony Davis

B) Stephen Curry and Klay Thompson

C) Kevin Durant and Kyrie Irving

D) James Harden and Russell Westbrook

12. How many first-round picks did the Brooklyn Nets make in the 2025 NBA Draft, a historic number for one team in a single draft?

A) Two

B) Three

C) Four

D) Five

13. Which Nets player from Croatia had his number 3 jersey retired after his career was tragically cut short in 1993?

A) Vince Carter
B) Drazen Petrovic
C) Deron Williams
D) Toni Kukoc

14. Which player did the Nets trade to the New York Knicks in 2024, reuniting him with his Villanova teammates?

A) Cam Thomas
B) Mikal Bridges
C) Ben Simmons
D) Spencer Dinwiddie

15. How many years were the Nets based in New Jersey before moving to Brooklyn?

A) 15 years
B) 25 years
C) 35 years
D) 45 years

Super Fan Secret Challenge

Only a true Nets fan will know this.

(No Answer Provided)

The Nets have played in many different arenas throughout their history. On the team's very first ABA game day in 1967, something went wrong with their home arena in Teaneck, New Jersey, that forced the game to be moved to a different location. What happened?

Answer Key

1. B) The American Basketball Association (ABA)

2. B) To rhyme with the Mets and Jets

3. B) Two

4. C) They needed money to pay the NBA merger fee

5. B) Vince Carter

6. B) Two

7. C) Jay-Z

8. C) 2012

9. B) The Notorious B.I.G.

10. C) Boston Celtics

11. C) Kevin Durant and Kyrie Irving

12. D) Five

13. B) Drazen Petrovic

14. B) Mikal Bridges

15. C) 35 years

NBA PLAYOFF BRACKET

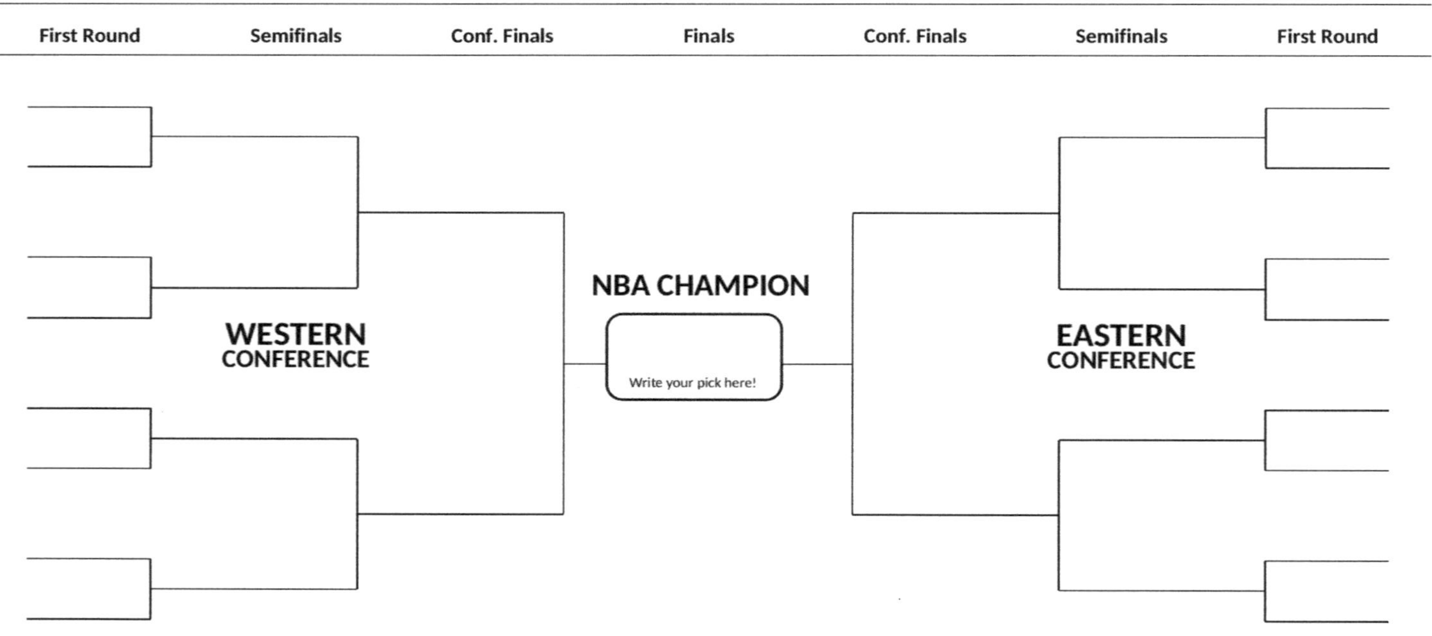

* Fill in your picks and try not to argue with your friends about it!

Part of the Fun Fan Facts: The Unofficial Sports Guide Series

Be the Boss of the Playoffs

You've broken down the matchups. You know which superstar takes over in the fourth quarter. You've seen the bench units that quietly decide series. You've watched the adjustments coaches make when their backs are against the wall.

Now it's time to stop watching and start deciding.

On this page, you are not just a fan. You are the Head Coach drawing up the last play with three seconds left on the clock. You are the GM who built this roster. You are the analyst who saw it all coming.

This is not just filling out a bracket.

This is building your championship run.

Sixteen teams enter the NBA Playoffs. The path is brutal. Best of seven. No shortcuts. No hiding. Every round gets louder, harder, and more personal.

This bracket is your Playoff Control Room.

The Game Plan

1. Survive Round One: Start with the opening round. Which matchup is going seven games? Who has the closer? Who folds under pressure? Make the calls.

2. Feel the Momentum: As you move into the Conference Semifinals and Conference Finals, things change. Role players become heroes. Stars feel the weight. Trust your reads.

3. Own the Finals: Trace your picks all the way to the NBA Finals. When the confetti falls and the trophy is raised, you'll find out who earned it.

House Rules: Circle your boldest upset. That is your official "I knew it" moment.

Choose Your Weapon: Pencil if you want flexibility. Pen if you trust your instincts. Sharpie if you believe in chaos.

Because once the playoffs tip off, there is no rewinding Game 7.

Make your picks. Trust your basketball brain. And let the playoff drama begin.

Fun Facts Wrap-Up

You made it through! You're officially a true superfan! Now it's time to put your knowledge to the test. Share these facts with friends and see who really knows their team best.

Love the series?

Your reviews help other fans discover Fun Fan Facts. If you enjoyed this book, we'd really appreciate you sharing your thoughts and leaving a review.

Want more Fun Fan Facts?

Scan the QR code below to visit our site and explore bonus trivia, challenges, and special extras - including new teams, future series, and collectible fun as they're released.

Collect All the Fun Fan Facts Series!

Check off every book you read. See the full set on Amazon. Search "Fun Fan Facts Jake Liam."

World Cup 2026 Edition

☐ Algeria   ☐ Scotland   ☐ Morocco

☐ France   ☐ Brazil   ☐ Switzerland

☐ Paraguay   ☐ Ivory Coast   ☐ Curaçao

☐ Argentina   ☐ Senegal   ☐ Netherlands

☐ Germany   ☐ Canada   ☐ Tunisia

☐ Portugal   ☐ Japan   ☐ Ecuador

☐ Australia   ☐ South Africa   ☐ New Zealand

☐ Ghana   ☐ Cape Verde   ☐ United States

☐ Qatar   ☐ Jordan   ☐ Egypt

☐ Austria   ☐ South Korea   ☐ Norway

☐ Haiti   ☐ Colombia   ☐ Uruguay

☐ Saudi Arabia   ☐ Mexico   ☐ England

☐ Belgium   ☐ Spain   ☐ Panama

☐ Iran   ☐ Croatia   ☐ Uzbekistan

World Cup 2026 Group Edition

☐ Group A   ☐ Group F   ☐ Group K

☐ Group E   ☐ Group J   ☐ Group D

☐ Group I   ☐ Group C   ☐ Group H

☐ Group B   ☐ Group G   ☐ Group L

English Football Edition

- ☐ Arsenal F.C.
- ☐ Aston Villa F.C.
- ☐ Chelsea F.C.
- ☐ Everton F.C.
- ☐ Fulham F.C.
- ☐ Liverpool F.C.
- ☐ Manchester City
- ☐ Manchester United
- ☐ Newcastle United F.C.
- ☐ Tottenham Hotspur
- ☐ West Ham United
- ☐ Wrexham A.F.C.

NBA Edition

- ☐ Atlanta Hawks
- ☐ Boston Celtics
- ☐ Brooklyn Nets
- ☐ Charlotte Hornets
- ☐ Chicago Bulls
- ☐ Cleveland Cavaliers
- ☐ Dallas Mavericks
- ☐ Denver Nuggets
- ☐ Detroit Pistons
- ☐ Golden State Warriors
- ☐ Houston Rockets
- ☐ Indiana Pacers
- ☐ LA Clippers
- ☐ Los Angeles Lakers
- ☐ Memphis Grizzlies
- ☐ Miami Heat
- ☐ Milwaukee Bucks
- ☐ Minnesota Timberwolves
- ☐ New Orleans Pelicans
- ☐ New York Knicks
- ☐ Oklahoma City Thunder
- ☐ Orlando Magic
- ☐ Philadelphia 76ers
- ☐ Phoenix Suns
- ☐ Portland Trail Blazers
- ☐ Sacramento Kings
- ☐ San Antonio Spurs
- ☐ Toronto Raptors
- ☐ Utah Jazz
- ☐ Washington Wizards

About the Author

Jake is a 13-year-old sports fan who loves football, American football, and basketball. He plays soccer as a goalie and dreams of one day playing for West Ham United and helping teach kids to love the game. His passion for sports runs in the family - his dad was a professional baseball player, and his stepdad sparked his love for West Ham. Through the Fun Fan Facts series, he shares the fun and excitement of sports with fans everywhere.

www.ingramcontent.com/pod-product-compliance
Lightning Source LLC
Chambersburg PA
CBHW050040040726
47599CB00015B/1772